THIS TEACHER PLANNER BELONGS TO:

TEACHER Information

CLASS #:

GRADE:

SCHOOL YEAR:

SCHOOL:

ADDRESS:

PHONE:

NOTES & MEMOS

RESOURCE LINKS

PERSONAL NOTES

SCHOOL Holidays

AUGUST	SEPTEMBER	OCTOBER

NOVEMBER	DECEMBER	NOTES

SCHOOL Holidays

JANUARY	FEBRUARY	MARCH

APRIL	MAY	JUNE

NOTES:

YEAR AT A *Glance*

AUGUST	SEPTEMBER	OCTOBER
NOVEMBER	DECEMBER	JANUARY
FEBRUARY	MARCH	APRIL
MAY	JUNE	

NOTES:

PARENT *Contacts*

STUDENT:
PARENTS:
PHONE #:
EMAIL:

STUDENT:
PARENTS:
PHONE #:
EMAIL:

STUDENT:
PARENTS:
PHONE #:
EMAIL:

STUDENT:
PARENTS:
PHONE #:
EMAIL:

STUDENT:
PARENTS:
PHONE #:
EMAIL:

STUDENT:
PARENTS:
PHONE #:
EMAIL:

STUDENT:
PARENTS:
PHONE #:
EMAIL:

STUDENT:
PARENTS:
PHONE #:
EMAIL:

STUDENT:
PARENTS:
PHONE #:
EMAIL:

STUDENT:
PARENTS:
PHONE #:
EMAIL:

PARENT *Contacts*

STUDENT:
PARENTS:
PHONE #:
EMAIL:

STUDENT:
PARENTS:
PHONE #:
EMAIL:

STUDENT:
PARENTS:
PHONE #:
EMAIL:

STUDENT:
PARENTS:
PHONE #:
EMAIL:

STUDENT:
PARENTS:
PHONE #:
EMAIL:

STUDENT:
PARENTS:
PHONE #:
EMAIL:

STUDENT:
PARENTS:
PHONE #:
EMAIL:

STUDENT:
PARENTS:
PHONE #:
EMAIL:

STUDENT:
PARENTS:
PHONE #:
EMAIL:

STUDENT:
PARENTS:
PHONE #:
EMAIL:

PARENT *Contacts*

STUDENT:
PARENTS:
PHONE #:
EMAIL:

STUDENT:
PARENTS:
PHONE #:
EMAIL:

STUDENT:
PARENTS:
PHONE #:
EMAIL:

STUDENT:
PARENTS:
PHONE #:
EMAIL:

STUDENT:
PARENTS:
PHONE #:
EMAIL:

STUDENT:
PARENTS:
PHONE #:
EMAIL:

STUDENT:
PARENTS:
PHONE #:
EMAIL:

STUDENT:
PARENTS:
PHONE #:
EMAIL:

STUDENT:
PARENTS:
PHONE #:
EMAIL:

STUDENT:
PARENTS:
PHONE #:
EMAIL:

PARENT CONTACT *Log*

MONTH:

NAME & DATE:	**REASON:**	**METHOD:**	**NOTES:**
		EMAIL: PHONE: MEETING:	
DATE:	**REASON:**	**METHOD:**	**NOTES:**
		EMAIL: PHONE: MEETING:	
DATE:	**REASON:**	**METHOD:**	**NOTES:**
		EMAIL: PHONE: MEETING:	
DATE:	**REASON:**	**METHOD:**	**NOTES:**
		EMAIL: PHONE: MEETING:	
DATE:	**REASON:**	**METHOD:**	**NOTES:**
		EMAIL: PHONE: MEETING:	

NOTES

PARENT CONTACT *Log*

MONTH:	

NAME & DATE:	**REASON:**	**METHOD:**	**NOTES:**
		EMAIL: PHONE: MEETING:	
DATE:	**REASON:**	**METHOD:**	**NOTES:**
		EMAIL: PHONE: MEETING:	
DATE:	**REASON:**	**METHOD:**	**NOTES:**
		EMAIL: PHONE: MEETING:	
DATE:	**REASON:**	**METHOD:**	**NOTES:**
		EMAIL: PHONE: MEETING:	
DATE:	**REASON:**	**METHOD:**	**NOTES:**
		EMAIL: PHONE: MEETING:	

NOTES

PARENT CONTACT *Log*

MONTH:

NAME & DATE:	**REASON:**	**METHOD:**	**NOTES:**
		EMAIL: PHONE: MEETING:	
DATE:	**REASON:**	**METHOD:**	**NOTES:**
		EMAIL: PHONE: MEETING:	
DATE:	**REASON:**	**METHOD:**	**NOTES:**
		EMAIL: PHONE: MEETING:	
DATE:	**REASON:**	**METHOD:**	**NOTES:**
		EMAIL: PHONE: MEETING:	
DATE:	**REASON:**	**METHOD:**	**NOTES:**
		EMAIL: PHONE: MEETING:	

NOTES

PARENT CONTACT *Log*

MONTH:

NAME & DATE: **REASON:** **METHOD:** **NOTES:**

EMAIL:

PHONE:

MEETING:

DATE: **REASON:** **METHOD:** **NOTES:**

EMAIL:

PHONE:

MEETING:

DATE: **REASON:** **METHOD:** **NOTES:**

EMAIL:

PHONE:

MEETING:

DATE: **REASON:** **METHOD:** **NOTES:**

EMAIL:

PHONE:

MEETING:

DATE: **REASON:** **METHOD:** **NOTES:**

EMAIL:

PHONE:

MEETING:

NOTES

PARENT CONTACT *Log*

MONTH:

NAME & DATE: **REASON:** **METHOD:** **NOTES:**

EMAIL:

PHONE:

MEETING:

DATE: **REASON:** **METHOD:** **NOTES:**

EMAIL:

PHONE:

MEETING:

DATE: **REASON:** **METHOD:** **NOTES:**

EMAIL:

PHONE:

MEETING:

DATE: **REASON:** **METHOD:** **NOTES:**

EMAIL:

PHONE:

MEETING:

DATE: **REASON:** **METHOD:** **NOTES:**

EMAIL:

PHONE:

MEETING:

NOTES

PARENT CONTACT *Log*

MONTH:	

NAME & DATE:	**REASON:**	**METHOD:**	**NOTES:**
		EMAIL: ☐ PHONE: ☐ MEETING: ☐	
DATE:	**REASON:**	**METHOD:**	**NOTES:**
		EMAIL: ☐ PHONE: ☐ MEETING: ☐	
DATE:	**REASON:**	**METHOD:**	**NOTES:**
		EMAIL: ☐ PHONE: ☐ MEETING: ☐	
DATE:	**REASON:**	**METHOD:**	**NOTES:**
		EMAIL: ☐ PHONE: ☐ MEETING: ☐	
DATE:	**REASON:**	**METHOD:**	**NOTES:**
		EMAIL: ☐ PHONE: ☐ MEETING: ☐	

NOTES

STUDENT Birthdays

AUGUST

SEPTEMBER

OCTOBER

NOVEMBER

DECEMBER

JANUARY

FEBRUARY

MARCH

APRIL

MAY

JUNE

CLASSROOM Expenses

MONTH: YEAR:

CLASS:

DATE	ITEM	DESCRIPTION	CATEGORY	COST

DATE:

CLASS Field Trip

EVENT

LOCATION

DEPT TIME:

RETURN TIME:

DATE:

TIME

TOTAL COST:

CONTACT

IMPORTANT Reminders

FIELD TRIP Checklist

Field Trip Itinerary

TIME:	ACTIVITIES:

PROGRESS Report

CLASS/SUBJECT:

DATE	SUBJECT/CLASS	LESSON PLAN #	ASSIGNMENTS

NOTES & IDEAS	ASSESSMENT

CUSTOMIZED ACTION PLAN

ASSIGNMENT Tracker

CLASS/SUBJECT: ______________________ WEEK OF: ______________________

MONDAY:	TUESDAY	WEDNESDAY

THURSDAY	FRIDAY	NOTES:

READING Tracker

CLASS:

BOOK TITLE: AUTHOR:

DATE	STUDENT	PAGES READ	NOTES

MONTHLY *Notes*

AUGUST				
M	T	W	T	F

NOTES, ACTIVITIES, PLANS & IDEAS

MONTHLY Schedule

CLASSROOM: **MONTH:**

M	T	W	T	F	S	S

NOTES, ACTIVITIES, PLANS & IDEAS

MONTHLY *Notes*

SEPTEMBER				
M	T	W	T	F

NOTES, ACTIVITIES, PLANS & IDEAS

MONTHLY Schedule

CLASSROOM: **MONTH:**

M	T	W	T	F	S	S

NOTES, ACTIVITIES, PLANS & IDEAS

MONTHLY *Notes*

OCTOBER				
M	T	W	T	F

NOTES, ACTIVITIES, PLANS & IDEAS

MONTHLY *Schedule*

CLASSROOM: **MONTH:**

M	T	W	T	F	S	S

NOTES, ACTIVITIES, PLANS & IDEAS

MONTHLY *Notes*

NOVEMBER				
M	T	W	T	F

NOTES, ACTIVITIES, PLANS & IDEAS

MONTHLY Schedule

CLASSROOM: **MONTH:**

M	T	W	T	F	S	S

NOTES, ACTIVITIES, PLANS & IDEAS

MONTHLY *Notes*

DECEMBER				
M	T	W	T	F

NOTES, ACTIVITIES, PLANS & IDEAS

MONTHLY *Schedule*

CLASSROOM: **MONTH:**

M	T	W	T	F	S	S

NOTES, ACTIVITIES, PLANS & IDEAS

MONTHLY *Notes*

JANUARY				
M	T	W	T	F

NOTES, ACTIVITIES, PLANS & IDEAS

MONTHLY Schedule

CLASSROOM: **MONTH:**

M	T	W	T	F	S	S

NOTES, ACTIVITIES, PLANS & IDEAS

MONTHLY *Notes*

FEBRUARY				
M	T	W	T	F

NOTES, ACTIVITIES, PLANS & IDEAS

MONTHLY Schedule

CLASSROOM: **MONTH:**

M	T	W	T	F	S	S

NOTES, ACTIVITIES, PLANS & IDEAS

MONTHLY Notes

MARCH				
M	T	W	T	F

NOTES, ACTIVITIES, PLANS & IDEAS

MONTHLY *Schedule*

CLASSROOM: **MONTH:**

M	T	W	T	F	S	S

NOTES, ACTIVITIES, PLANS & IDEAS

MONTHLY Notes

APRIL				
M	T	W	T	F

NOTES, ACTIVITIES, PLANS & IDEAS

MONTHLY Schedule

CLASSROOM: **MONTH:**

M	T	W	T	F	S	S

NOTES, ACTIVITIES, PLANS & IDEAS

MONTHLY Notes

MAY				
M	T	W	T	F

NOTES, ACTIVITIES, PLANS & IDEAS

MONTHLY Schedule

CLASSROOM: **MONTH:**

M	T	W	T	F	S	S

NOTES, ACTIVITIES, PLANS & IDEAS

MONTHLY Notes

JUNE				
M	T	W	T	F

NOTES, ACTIVITIES, PLANS & IDEAS

MONTHLY Schedule

CLASSROOM: **MONTH:**

M	T	W	T	F	S	S

NOTES, ACTIVITIES, PLANS & IDEAS

DATE:

WEEKLY ROLL *Call*

FIRST NAME:	LAST NAME:	STATUS:

WEEKLY *Overview*

WEEK OF: ....

MONDAY

TUESDAY

WEDNESDAY

THURSDAY

FRIDAY

SATURDAY

SUNDAY

IMPORTANT NOTES

WEEKLY *Lesson Plan*

MONDAY

EQ/ I CAN NOTES:

TUESDAY

EQ/ I CAN NOTES:

WEDNESDAY

EQ/ I CAN NOTES:

THURSDAY

EQ/ I CAN NOTES:

FRIDAY

EQ/ I CAN NOTES:

CLASS Projects

PROJECT TITLE:

DETAILS:

START DATE: **DUE DATE:**

DATE	TASK COMPLETED

READING Tracker

CLASS:

BOOK TITLE: AUTHOR:

DATE	STUDENT	PAGES READ	NOTES

WEEKLY *Planner*

MONDAY

TUESDAY

WEDNESDAY

THURSDAY

FRIDAY

EQ/I CAN NOTES:

LESSON Planner

SUBJECT:

DATE:

UNIT:

OBJECTIVE:

LESSON:

OVERVIEW

TOPICS COVERED

ASSIGNMENTS

NOTES

ASSIGNMENT Tracker

CLASS/SUBJECT: ____________ WEEK OF: ____________

MONDAY:

TUESDAY

WEDNESDAY

THURSDAY

FRIDAY

NOTES:

DAILY Schedule

TO DO LIST:

DATE

6 AM

7 AM

8 AM

9 AM

10 AM

11 AM

12 PM

1 PM

2 PM

3 PM

4 PM

5 PM

REMINDERS:

6 PM

7 PM

8 PM

NOTES:

9 PM

10 PM

NOTES

DAY PLANNER *Monday*

DATE:

5am:

6am:

7am:

8am:

9am:

10am:

11am:

12pm:

1pm:

2pm:

3pm:

4pm:

DAILY TO DO LIST:

DAILY GOALS:

NOTES & REMINDERS:

DAY PLANNER

DATE:

5am:

6am:

7am:

8am:

9am:

10am:

11am:

12pm:

1pm:

2pm:

3pm:

4pm:

DAILY TO DO LIST:

DAILY GOALS:

NOTES & REMINDERS:

DAY PLANNER *Wednesday*

DATE:

5am:

6am:

7am:

8am:

9am:

10am:

11am:

12pm:

1pm:

2pm:

3pm:

4pm:

DAILY TO DO LIST:

DAILY GOALS:

NOTES & REMINDERS:

DAY PLANNER *Thursday*

DATE:

5am:

6am:

7am:

8am:

9am:

10am:

11am:

12pm:

1pm:

2pm:

3pm:

4pm:

DAILY TO DO LIST:

DAILY GOALS:

NOTES & REMINDERS:

DAY PLANNER

DATE:

5am:

6am:

7am:

8am:

9am:

10am:

11am:

12pm:

1pm:

2pm:

3pm:

4pm:

DAILY TO DO LIST:

DAILY GOALS:

NOTES & REMINDERS:

DATE:

WEEKLY ROLL *Call*

FIRST NAME: LAST NAME: STATUS:

WEEKLY *Overview*

WEEK OF: ....

MONDAY

TUESDAY

WEDNESDAY

THURSDAY

FRIDAY

SATURDAY

SUNDAY

IMPORTANT NOTES

WEEKLY Lesson Plan

MONDAY

EQ/ I CAN NOTES:

TUESDAY

EQ/ I CAN NOTES:

WEDNESDAY

EQ/ I CAN NOTES:

THURSDAY

EQ/ I CAN NOTES:

FRIDAY

EQ/ I CAN NOTES:

READING Tracker

CLASS:

BOOK TITLE: **AUTHOR:**

DATE	STUDENT	PAGES READ	NOTES

LESSON *Planner*

SUBJECT:

UNIT:

LESSON:

DATE:

OBJECTIVE:

OVERVIEW

TOPICS COVERED

ASSIGNMENTS

NOTES

DAY PLANNER *Monday*

DATE:

5am:

6am:

7am:

8am:

9am:

10am:

11am:

12pm:

1pm:

2pm:

3pm:

4pm:

DAILY TO DO LIST:

DAILY GOALS:

NOTES & REMINDERS:

DAY PLANNER

DATE:

5am:

6am:

7am:

8am:

9am:

10am:

11am:

12pm:

1pm:

2pm:

3pm:

4pm:

DAILY TO DO LIST:

DAILY GOALS:

NOTES & REMINDERS:

DAY PLANNER *Wednesday*

DATE:

5am:

6am:

7am:

8am:

9am:

10am:

11am:

12pm:

1pm:

2pm:

3pm:

4pm:

DAILY TO DO LIST:

DAILY GOALS:

NOTES & REMINDERS:

DAY PLANNER *Thursday*

DATE:

5am:

6am:

7am:

8am:

9am:

10am:

11am:

12pm:

1pm:

2pm:

3pm:

4pm:

DAILY TO DO LIST:

DAILY GOALS:

NOTES & REMINDERS:

DAY PLANNER

DATE:

5am:

6am:

7am:

8am:

9am:

10am:

11am:

12pm:

1pm:

2pm:

3pm:

4pm:

DAILY TO DO LIST:

DAILY GOALS:

NOTES & REMINDERS:

DATE:

WEEKLY ROLL *Call*

FIRST NAME:	LAST NAME:	STATUS:

WEEKLY Overview

WEEK OF: ....

MONDAY

TUESDAY

WEDNESDAY

THURSDAY

FRIDAY

SATURDAY

SUNDAY

IMPORTANT NOTES

WEEKLY Lesson Plan

MONDAY

EQ/ I CAN NOTES:

TUESDAY

EQ/ I CAN NOTES:

WEDNESDAY

EQ/ I CAN NOTES:

THURSDAY

EQ/ I CAN NOTES:

FRIDAY

EQ/ I CAN NOTES:

READING Tracker

CLASS:

BOOK TITLE: AUTHOR:

DATE	STUDENT	PAGES READ	NOTES

LESSON Planner

SUBJECT:

UNIT:

LESSON:

DATE:

OBJECTIVE:

OVERVIEW

TOPICS COVERED

ASSIGNMENTS

NOTES

DAY PLANNER *Monday*

DATE:

5am:

6am:

7am:

8am:

9am:

10am:

11am:

12pm:

1pm:

2pm:

3pm:

4pm:

DAILY TO DO LIST:

DAILY GOALS:

NOTES & REMINDERS:

DAY PLANNER

DATE:

5am:

6am:

7am:

8am:

9am:

10am:

11am:

12pm:

1pm:

2pm:

3pm:

4pm:

DAILY TO DO LIST:

DAILY GOALS:

NOTES & REMINDERS:

DAY PLANNER *Wednesday*

DATE:

5am:

6am:

7am:

8am:

9am:

10am:

11am:

12pm:

1pm:

2pm:

3pm:

4pm:

DAILY TO DO LIST:

DAILY GOALS:

NOTES & REMINDERS:

DAY PLANNER Thursday

DATE:

5am:

6am:

7am:

8am:

9am:

10am:

11am:

12pm:

1pm:

2pm:

3pm:

4pm:

DAILY TO DO LIST:

DAILY GOALS:

NOTES & REMINDERS:

DAY PLANNER 

DATE:

5am:

6am:

7am:

8am:

9am:

10am:

11am:

12pm:

1pm:

2pm:

3pm:

4pm:

DAILY TO DO LIST:

DAILY GOALS:

NOTES & REMINDERS:

DATE:

WEEKLY ROLL *Call*

FIRST NAME:	LAST NAME:	STATUS:

WEEKLY Overview

WEEK OF: ....

MONDAY	TUESDAY	WEDNESDAY

THURSDAY	FRIDAY	SATURDAY

SUNDAY	IMPORTANT NOTES

WEEKLY Lesson Plan

MONDAY

EQ/ I CAN NOTES:

TUESDAY

EQ/ I CAN NOTES:

WEDNESDAY

EQ/ I CAN NOTES:

THURSDAY

EQ/ I CAN NOTES:

FRIDAY

EQ/ I CAN NOTES:

READING Tracker

CLASS:

BOOK TITLE:

AUTHOR:

DATE	STUDENT	PAGES READ	NOTES

LESSON Planner

SUBJECT:

DATE:

UNIT:

OBJECTIVE:

LESSON:

OVERVIEW

TOPICS COVERED

ASSIGNMENTS

NOTES

DAY PLANNER *Monday*

DATE:

5am:

6am:

7am:

8am:

9am:

10am:

11am:

12pm:

1pm:

2pm:

3pm:

4pm:

DAILY TO DO LIST:

DAILY GOALS:

NOTES & REMINDERS:

DAY PLANNER

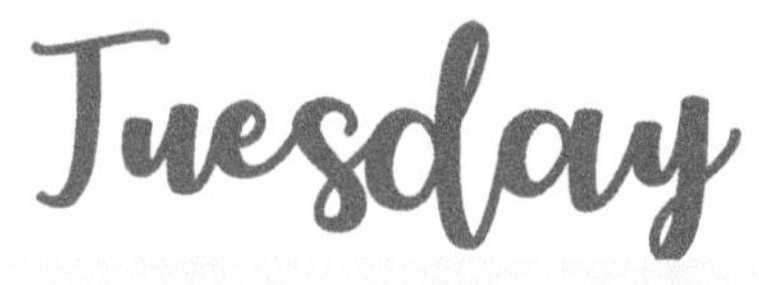

DATE:

5am:

6am:

7am:

8am:

9am:

10am:

11am:

12pm:

1pm:

2pm:

3pm:

4pm:

DAILY TO DO LIST:

DAILY GOALS:

NOTES & REMINDERS:

DAY PLANNER *Wednesday*

DATE:

5am:

6am:

7am:

8am:

9am:

10am:

11am:

12pm:

1pm:

2pm:

3pm:

4pm:

DAILY TO DO LIST:

DAILY GOALS:

NOTES & REMINDERS:

DAY PLANNER *Thursday*

DATE:

5am:

6am:

7am:

8am:

9am:

10am:

11am:

12pm:

1pm:

2pm:

3pm:

4pm:

DAILY TO DO LIST:

DAILY GOALS:

NOTES & REMINDERS:

DAY PLANNER

DATE:

5am:

6am:

7am:

8am:

9am:

10am:

11am:

12pm:

1pm:

2pm:

3pm:

4pm:

DAILY TO DO LIST:

DAILY GOALS:

NOTES & REMINDERS:

DATE:

WEEKLY ROLL *Call*

FIRST NAME:	LAST NAME:	STATUS:

WEEKLY *Overview*

WEEK OF: ....

MONDAY

TUESDAY

WEDNESDAY

THURSDAY

FRIDAY

SATURDAY

SUNDAY

IMPORTANT NOTES

WEEKLY Lesson Plan

MONDAY

EQ/ I CAN NOTES:

TUESDAY

EQ/ I CAN NOTES:

WEDNESDAY

EQ/ I CAN NOTES:

THURSDAY

EQ/ I CAN NOTES:

FRIDAY

EQ/ I CAN NOTES:

READING *Tracker*

CLASS:

BOOK TITLE: AUTHOR:

DATE	STUDENT	PAGES READ	NOTES

LESSON *Planner*

SUBJECT:

DATE:

UNIT:

OBJECTIVE:

LESSON:

OVERVIEW

TOPICS COVERED

ASSIGNMENTS

NOTES

DAY PLANNER *Monday*

DATE:

5am:

6am:

7am:

8am:

9am:

10am:

11am:

12pm:

1pm:

2pm:

3pm:

4pm:

DAILY TO DO LIST:

DAILY GOALS:

NOTES & REMINDERS:

DAY PLANNER

DATE:

5am:

6am:

7am:

8am:

9am:

10am:

11am:

12pm:

1pm:

2pm:

3pm:

4pm:

DAILY TO DO LIST:

DAILY GOALS:

NOTES & REMINDERS:

DAY PLANNER *Wednesday*

DATE:

5am:

6am:

7am:

8am:

9am:

10am:

11am:

12pm:

1pm:

2pm:

3pm:

4pm:

DAILY TO DO LIST:

DAILY GOALS:

NOTES & REMINDERS:

DAY PLANNER *Thursday*

DATE:

5am:

6am:

7am:

8am:

9am:

10am:

11am:

12pm:

1pm:

2pm:

3pm:

4pm:

DAILY TO DO LIST:

DAILY GOALS:

NOTES & REMINDERS:

DAY PLANNER 

DATE:

5am:

6am:

7am:

8am:

9am:

10am:

11am:

12pm:

1pm:

2pm:

3pm:

4pm:

DAILY TO DO LIST:

DAILY GOALS:

NOTES & REMINDERS:

DATE:

WEEKLY ROLL *Call*

FIRST NAME: LAST NAME: STATUS:

WEEKLY Overview

WEEK OF: ....

MONDAY

TUESDAY

WEDNESDAY

THURSDAY

FRIDAY

SATURDAY

SUNDAY

IMPORTANT NOTES

WEEKLY Lesson Plan

MONDAY

EQ/ I CAN NOTES:

TUESDAY

EQ/ I CAN NOTES:

WEDNESDAY

EQ/ I CAN NOTES:

THURSDAY

EQ/ I CAN NOTES:

FRIDAY

EQ/ I CAN NOTES:

READING Tracker

CLASS:

BOOK TITLE: **AUTHOR:**

DATE	STUDENT	PAGES READ	NOTES

LESSON *Planner*

SUBJECT:

DATE:

UNIT:

OBJECTIVE:

LESSON:

OVERVIEW

TOPICS COVERED

ASSIGNMENTS

NOTES

DAY PLANNER *Monday*

DATE:

5am:

6am:

7am:

8am:

9am:

10am:

11am:

12pm:

1pm:

2pm:

3pm:

4pm:

DAILY TO DO LIST:

DAILY GOALS:

NOTES & REMINDERS:

DAY PLANNER

DATE:

5am:

6am:

7am:

8am:

9am:

10am:

11am:

12pm:

1pm:

2pm:

3pm:

4pm:

DAILY TO DO LIST:

DAILY GOALS:

NOTES & REMINDERS:

DAY PLANNER Wednesday

DATE:

5am:

6am:

7am:

8am:

9am:

10am:

11am:

12pm:

1pm:

2pm:

3pm:

4pm:

DAILY TO DO LIST:

DAILY GOALS:

NOTES & REMINDERS:

DAY PLANNER *Thursday*

DATE:

5am:

6am:

7am:

8am:

9am:

10am:

11am:

12pm:

1pm:

2pm:

3pm:

4pm:

DAILY TO DO LIST:

DAILY GOALS:

NOTES & REMINDERS:

DAY PLANNER

DATE:

5am:

6am:

7am:

8am:

9am:

10am:

11am:

12pm:

1pm:

2pm:

3pm:

4pm:

DAILY TO DO LIST:

DAILY GOALS:

NOTES & REMINDERS:

DATE:

WEEKLY ROLL *Call*

FIRST NAME:	LAST NAME:	STATUS:

WEEKLY *Overview*

WEEK OF: ....

MONDAY

TUESDAY

WEDNESDAY

THURSDAY

FRIDAY

SATURDAY

SUNDAY

IMPORTANT NOTES

WEEKLY Lesson Plan

MONDAY

EQ/ I CAN NOTES:

TUESDAY

EQ/ I CAN NOTES:

WEDNESDAY

EQ/ I CAN NOTES:

THURSDAY

EQ/ I CAN NOTES:

FRIDAY

EQ/ I CAN NOTES:

READING Tracker

CLASS:

BOOK TITLE: AUTHOR:

DATE	STUDENT	PAGES READ	NOTES

LESSON *Planner*

SUBJECT:

DATE:

UNIT:

OBJECTIVE:

LESSON:

OVERVIEW

TOPICS COVERED

ASSIGNMENTS

NOTES

DAY PLANNER *Monday*

DATE:

5am:

6am:

7am:

8am:

9am:

10am:

11am:

12pm:

1pm:

2pm:

3pm:

4pm:

DAILY TO DO LIST:

DAILY GOALS:

NOTES & REMINDERS:

DAY PLANNER

DATE:

5am:

6am:

7am:

8am:

9am:

10am:

11am:

12pm:

1pm:

2pm:

3pm:

4pm:

DAILY TO DO LIST:

DAILY GOALS:

NOTES & REMINDERS:

DAY PLANNER *Wednesday*

DATE:

5am:

6am:

7am:

8am:

9am:

10am:

11am:

12pm:

1pm:

2pm:

3pm:

4pm:

DAILY TO DO LIST:

DAILY GOALS:

NOTES & REMINDERS:

DAY PLANNER *Thursday*

DATE:

5am:

6am:

7am:

8am:

9am:

10am:

11am:

12pm:

1pm:

2pm:

3pm:

4pm:

DAILY TO DO LIST:

DAILY GOALS:

NOTES & REMINDERS:

DAY PLANNER 

DATE:

5am:

6am:

7am:

8am:

9am:

10am:

11am:

12pm:

1pm:

2pm:

3pm:

4pm:

DAILY TO DO LIST:

DAILY GOALS:

NOTES & REMINDERS:

DATE:

WEEKLY ROLL *Call*

FIRST NAME:	LAST NAME:	STATUS:

WEEKLY Overview

WEEK OF: ....

MONDAY

TUESDAY

WEDNESDAY

THURSDAY

FRIDAY

SATURDAY

SUNDAY

IMPORTANT NOTES

WEEKLY Lesson Plan

MONDAY

EQ/ I CAN NOTES:

TUESDAY

EQ/ I CAN NOTES:

WEDNESDAY

EQ/ I CAN NOTES:

THURSDAY

EQ/ I CAN NOTES:

FRIDAY

EQ/ I CAN NOTES:

READING Tracker

CLASS:

BOOK TITLE: AUTHOR:

DATE	STUDENT	PAGES READ	NOTES

LESSON Planner

SUBJECT:

UNIT:

LESSON:

DATE:

OBJECTIVE:

OVERVIEW

TOPICS COVERED

ASSIGNMENTS

NOTES

DAY PLANNER *Monday*

DATE:

5am:

6am:

7am:

8am:

9am:

10am:

11am:

12pm:

1pm:

2pm:

3pm:

4pm:

DAILY TO DO LIST:

DAILY GOALS:

NOTES & REMINDERS:

DAY PLANNER

DATE:

5am:

6am:

7am:

8am:

9am:

10am:

11am:

12pm:

1pm:

2pm:

3pm:

4pm:

DAILY TO DO LIST:

DAILY GOALS:

NOTES & REMINDERS:

DAY PLANNER *Wednesday*

DATE:

5am:

6am:

7am:

8am:

9am:

10am:

11am:

12pm:

1pm:

2pm:

3pm:

4pm:

DAILY TO DO LIST:

DAILY GOALS:

NOTES & REMINDERS:

DAY PLANNER *Thursday*

DATE:

5am:

6am:

7am:

8am:

9am:

10am:

11am:

12pm:

1pm:

2pm:

3pm:

4pm:

DAILY TO DO LIST:

DAILY GOALS:

NOTES & REMINDERS:

DAY PLANNER

DATE:

5am:

6am:

7am:

8am:

9am:

10am:

11am:

12pm:

1pm:

2pm:

3pm:

4pm:

DAILY TO DO LIST:

DAILY GOALS:

NOTES & REMINDERS:

DATE:

WEEKLY ROLL *Call*

FIRST NAME: LAST NAME: STATUS:

WEEKLY Overview

WEEK OF: ....

MONDAY

TUESDAY

WEDNESDAY

THURSDAY

FRIDAY

SATURDAY

SUNDAY

IMPORTANT NOTES

WEEKLY Lesson Plan

MONDAY

EQ/ I CAN NOTES:

TUESDAY

EQ/ I CAN NOTES:

WEDNESDAY

EQ/ I CAN NOTES:

THURSDAY

EQ/ I CAN NOTES:

FRIDAY

EQ/ I CAN NOTES:

READING Tracker

CLASS:

BOOK TITLE: AUTHOR:

DATE	STUDENT	PAGES READ	NOTES

LESSON *Planner*

SUBJECT:

UNIT:

LESSON:

DATE:

OBJECTIVE:

OVERVIEW

TOPICS COVERED

ASSIGNMENTS

NOTES

DAY PLANNER *Monday*

DATE:

5am:

6am:

7am:

8am:

9am:

10am:

11am:

12pm:

1pm:

2pm:

3pm:

4pm:

DAILY TO DO LIST:

DAILY GOALS:

NOTES & REMINDERS:

DAY PLANNER

DATE:

5am:

6am:

7am:

8am:

9am:

10am:

11am:

12pm:

1pm:

2pm:

3pm:

4pm:

DAILY TO DO LIST:

DAILY GOALS:

NOTES & REMINDERS:

DAY PLANNER *Wednesday*

DATE:

5am:

6am:

7am:

8am:

9am:

10am:

11am:

12pm:

1pm:

2pm:

3pm:

4pm:

DAILY TO DO LIST:

DAILY GOALS:

NOTES & REMINDERS:

DAY PLANNER *Thursday*

DATE:

5am:

6am:

7am:

8am:

9am:

10am:

11am:

12pm:

1pm:

2pm:

3pm:

4pm:

DAILY TO DO LIST:

DAILY GOALS:

NOTES & REMINDERS:

DAY PLANNER 

DATE:

5am:

6am:

7am:

8am:

9am:

10am:

11am:

12pm:

1pm:

2pm:

3pm:

4pm:

DAILY TO DO LIST:

DAILY GOALS:

NOTES & REMINDERS:

PARENT-TEACHER *Meetings*

STUDENT NAME:

DATE & TIME:

REASON FOR MEETING

TOPICS DISCUSSED

ACTION PLAN & GOALS

STUDENT NAME:

DATE & TIME:

REASON FOR MEETING

TOPICS DISCUSSED

ACTION PLAN & GOALS

STUDENT *Information*

STUDENT INFORMATION

NAME:

BIRTH DATE:

ADDRESS:

PARENTS NAMES:

PHONE:

EMAIL ADDRESS:

ACADEMIC HISTORY

STUDENT ID:

CHALLENGES:

STRENGTHS:

MEDICAL INFORMATION

PRIMARY CONTACT INFORMATION

EMERGENCY CONTACT INFORMATION

ADDITIONAL INFORMATION

STUDENT *Information*

STUDENT INFORMATION

NAME:

BIRTH DATE:

ADDRESS:

PARENTS NAMES:

PHONE:

EMAIL ADDRESS:

ACADEMIC HISTORY

STUDENT ID:

CHALLENGES:

STRENGTHS:

MEDICAL INFORMATION

PRIMARY CONTACT INFORMATION

EMERGENCY CONTACT INFORMATION

ADDITIONAL INFORMATION

STUDENT *Information*

STUDENT INFORMATION

NAME:

ADDRESS:

PHONE:

BIRTH DATE:

PARENTS NAMES:

EMAIL ADDRESS:

ACADEMIC HISTORY

STUDENT ID:

CHALLENGES:

STRENGTHS:

MEDICAL INFORMATION

PRIMARY CONTACT INFORMATION

EMERGENCY CONTACT INFORMATION

ADDITIONAL INFORMATION

STUDENT *Information*

STUDENT INFORMATION

NAME: BIRTH DATE:

ADDRESS: PARENTS NAMES:

PHONE: EMAIL ADDRESS:

ACADEMIC HISTORY

STUDENT ID:

CHALLENGES:

STRENGTHS:

MEDICAL INFORMATION

PRIMARY CONTACT INFORMATION

EMERGENCY CONTACT INFORMATION

ADDITIONAL INFORMATION

STUDENT *Information*

STUDENT INFORMATION

NAME:

BIRTH DATE:

ADDRESS:

PARENTS NAMES:

PHONE:

EMAIL ADDRESS:

ACADEMIC HISTORY

STUDENT ID:

CHALLENGES:

STRENGTHS:

MEDICAL INFORMATION

PRIMARY CONTACT INFORMATION

EMERGENCY CONTACT INFORMATION

ADDITIONAL INFORMATION

STUDENT *Information*

STUDENT INFORMATION

NAME:

BIRTH DATE:

ADDRESS:

PARENTS NAMES:

PHONE:

EMAIL ADDRESS:

ACADEMIC HISTORY

STUDENT ID:

CHALLENGES:

STRENGTHS:

MEDICAL INFORMATION

PRIMARY CONTACT INFORMATION

EMERGENCY CONTACT INFORMATION

ADDITIONAL INFORMATION

STUDENT *Information*

STUDENT INFORMATION

NAME:

BIRTH DATE:

ADDRESS:

PARENTS NAMES:

PHONE:

EMAIL ADDRESS:

ACADEMIC HISTORY

STUDENT ID:

CHALLENGES:

STRENGTHS:

MEDICAL INFORMATION

PRIMARY CONTACT INFORMATION

EMERGENCY CONTACT INFORMATION

ADDITIONAL INFORMATION

STUDENT *Information*

STUDENT INFORMATION

NAME:

BIRTH DATE:

ADDRESS:

PARENTS NAMES:

PHONE:

EMAIL ADDRESS:

ACADEMIC HISTORY

STUDENT ID:

CHALLENGES:

STRENGTHS:

MEDICAL INFORMATION

PRIMARY CONTACT INFORMATION

EMERGENCY CONTACT INFORMATION

ADDITIONAL INFORMATION

STUDENT Information

STUDENT INFORMATION

NAME:

ADDRESS:

PHONE:

BIRTH DATE:

PARENTS NAMES:

EMAIL ADDRESS:

ACADEMIC HISTORY

STUDENT ID:

CHALLENGES:

STRENGTHS:

MEDICAL INFORMATION

PRIMARY CONTACT INFORMATION

EMERGENCY CONTACT INFORMATION

ADDITIONAL INFORMATION

STUDENT Information

STUDENT INFORMATION

NAME:

BIRTH DATE:

ADDRESS:

PARENTS NAMES:

PHONE:

EMAIL ADDRESS:

ACADEMIC HISTORY

STUDENT ID:

CHALLENGES:

STRENGTHS:

MEDICAL INFORMATION

PRIMARY CONTACT INFORMATION

EMERGENCY CONTACT INFORMATION

ADDITIONAL INFORMATION

STUDENT Information

STUDENT INFORMATION

NAME:

BIRTH DATE:

ADDRESS:

PARENTS NAMES:

PHONE:

EMAIL ADDRESS:

ACADEMIC HISTORY

STUDENT ID:

CHALLENGES:

STRENGTHS:

MEDICAL INFORMATION

PRIMARY CONTACT INFORMATION

EMERGENCY CONTACT INFORMATION

ADDITIONAL INFORMATION

STUDENT Information

STUDENT INFORMATION

NAME:

BIRTH DATE:

ADDRESS:

PARENTS NAMES:

PHONE:

EMAIL ADDRESS:

ACADEMIC HISTORY

STUDENT ID:

CHALLENGES:

STRENGTHS:

MEDICAL INFORMATION

PRIMARY CONTACT INFORMATION

EMERGENCY CONTACT INFORMATION

ADDITIONAL INFORMATION